CONFESSION

Moreno Dal Bello

CONFESSION

"That the doctrine of confession has caused difficulties for the (Roman) Catholic Church, in one way or another, is unchallenged. After mentioning the 'countless attacks' upon this teaching, 'The Catholic Encyclopedia' remarked: 'If at the Reformation or since the (Roman Catholic) Church could have surrendered a doctrine or abandoned a practice for the sake of peace and to soften a 'hard saying', confession would have been the first to disappear.'" **R.E. Woodrow**

WHAT IS CONFESSION? –
THE ROMAN CATHOLIC VIEW

The Baltimore Catechism defines confession as simply *"...the telling of our sins to an authorized priest for the purpose of obtaining forgiveness."*[1] Another of Rome's Catechisms states that *"Sins are forgiven by the power of God, which Jesus Christ has given to the priests of His Church."*[2] The French Catechism goes even further in its description of confession, claiming that *"One must receive absolution in feelings of total humility, considering the confessor (the priest), as Jesus Christ Himself whose place he takes."*

It is taught that the confession of one's sins to a priest, one of 6 commandments decreed by the Roman Catholic Church, should be made at least once a year. We are told that confession, in order to be valid, must be spoken into the ear of a priest; this is termed **'auricular confession'**. *"In the Roman system the priest constantly comes between the sinner and God. In...the New Catechism No. 1, with imprimatur by Cardinal **Francis Spellman**, of New York, we read: 'You must tell your sins to the priest to have them forgiven.' And again, 'Confession is telling your sins to the priest to obtain forgiveness.'"*[3]

The Roman Catholic Church says of Jesus Christ: *"He who forgave sins so readily while He was on earth continues to do so. Now He does it through the ministry of the priests in the sacrament of penance."*[4]

"...this confession is made by every individual, in SECRECY AND IN SOLITUDE, to the priest sitting in the name, and clothed with the authority, of God, invested with the power to examine the conscience, to judge the life, to absolve or condemn according to his mere arbitrary will and pleasure. This is the grand pivot on which the whole 'Mystery of iniquity', as embodied in the Papacy, is made to turn; and wherever it is submitted to, admirably does it serve the design of binding men in abject subjection to the priesthood."[5]

The book, *'Instructions for Non-Catholics'*, written primarily for those in the process of converting to Roman Catholicism, boldly declares: *"The priest does not have to ask God to forgive your sins. The priest himself has the power to do so in Christ's name. Your sins are forgiven by the priest the same as if you knelt before Jesus Christ and told them to Christ Himself."*

Roman Catholics are taught to confess all their mortal sins to the priest who, ironically, although able to 'forgive their sin', cannot remit the punishment due to those allegedly 'forgiven' sins. The Baltimore Catechism specifies that *"When we have committed no mortal sins since our last confession, we should confess our venial* (less serious) *sins or some sin told in a previous confession for which we are again sorry, in order that the priest may give us absolution."*[6]

Roman Catholicism teaches that any sin that is not confessed is not forgiven. Even the omission of one sin may invalidate the entire confession. This is in contrast with the inspired words of David in Psalm 19:13 where he says, **"...cleanse me from my unknown faults"**, undeniably implying that it is *humanly impossible* for a man to be aware of all his sins, let alone confess them.

Amazingly, *"According to a decree of the Council of Trent it is not necessary, in order to obtain pardon in the confessional, that the sinner be sorry because his sin was an offence against God, <u>but only that he be sorry for fear that unless he confesses before a priest and receives forgiveness he will go to hell forever.</u> The decree reads: 'It is sufficient if he is sorry for fear of otherwise burning in hell for all eternity.'"*[7]

Many Roman Catholics prefer to confess their sins regularly to the same priest. The more devout followers attending the confessional once a month and others as frequently as once a week. Bishop **Hay** asks the question: *"Is this confession (to the priest) necessary for obtaining absolution?"* He confidently responds: *"It is ordained by Jesus Christ as <u>absolutely necessary for this purpose."</u>*[8] Now just where Bishop **Hay** gets his evidence to support this non-biblical claim is a mystery. He certainly does not get it from the Bible.

Children as young as 7 are required to begin confessing their sins to a priest, who is said to be a mediator between God and man; a claim that, as shall be looked at later in more detail, is completely rejected by the Roman Catholic Bible, which plainly declares that Jesus Christ is the ONE and ONLY Mediator between God and man.

THE CONFESSIONAL

Confession, as practiced by the Roman Catholic Church, customarily takes place in what is called a 'confessional box'—a partitioned, dimly lit, wooden structure, which may be found in every Roman Catholic Church. On occasion, however, confessions are conducted in the confessant's home and may even take place in a priest's private rooms.

After having entered the confessional, one kneels before the priest and commences his 'confession' with the words: *'Bless me father for I have sinned; it has been 'several' weeks since my last confession father, and these are my sins...'* In some churches, what is known as the *Confiteor* is recited before the confession is made. The Confiteor consists, in part, of the following: *"I confess to Almighty God, to the blessed virgin Mary, to blessed Michael the archangel, to blessed John the Baptist, to the holy apostles Peter and Paul, to all the saints and to you father* (referring to the priest)*..."* Note that there is no reference made at all, in this avowal, to the Lord Jesus Christ and that the confession is made *equally* to God, Mary, an archangel and to mere men.

The confessant is then required to name his sins as well as the number of times they were committed. The priest may, and often does, ask questions probing the sinner for more detail in order that a 'full and proper confession' be made. The priest then prays, gives a blessing and 'absolves' the sinner of his sins saying, *"I absolve you from your sins in the name of the Father, and of the Son, and of the Holy Ghost. Amen."* The priest then assigns him penance, usually made up of the Lord's Prayer and several Hail Mary's.

"Acts of penance can include restitution, recitation of certain prayers, self-denial, bodily affliction, and prescribed devotional exercises. However, temporal punishment and penance due to confessed and forgiven sin can also be satisfied by means of indulgences."[9]

THE ORIGIN AND HISTORY OF (AURICULAR) CONFESSION

Something that by now should not come as any surprise to Roman Catholics is the fact that, as with the rosary, purgatory and baptism, the whole concept of confessing one's sins to a priest did not originate within the Roman Catholic Church, but emanates from the heart of Babylon. The Babylonian system of secret confession to a priest was required of all those who wished to be admitted to the 'Mysteries' of that pagan system.

Once this confession was made, the confessant came under the power of the priest. This Babylonian system is indistinguishable from that of the Roman Catholic Church today. *"Without such confession, in the Church of Rome, there can be no admission to the Sacraments, any more than in the days of Paganism there could be admission without confession to the benefit of the Mysteries."*[10]

This concept of confession to a priest was not only practiced in Babylon but also later found among the Greeks. Some of the pagan priests of ancient Greece, called Köes, often heard confessions and were said to have 'purged the guilt away'. Certain types of confession were also taught in the religions of Medo-Persia, Egypt and Rome long before the commencement of Christianity.

The pagan concept of auricular confession operated under the pretence that the mysteries, which the initiate was to be admitted to, were so high and holy that no man with a guilty conscience or unpurged sin could be lawfully admitted. Therefore, *"For the safety....of those who were to be initiated, it was held to be indispensable that the officiating priest should thoroughly probe their consciences, lest coming without due purgation from previous guilt contracted, the wrath of the gods should be provoked against the profane intruders."*[11] The Roman Catholic Church has evidently continued this pagan practice and, as we shall see shortly, justified it by a perverted use of the Scriptures.

What has escaped the notice of most Roman Catholics is the fact that no authorization was ever given, nor was this auricular confession practiced during the first 1,000 years of Christianity! The early 'Church fathers' knew nothing of the concept. Confession was taught in accordance with Holy Scripture, with sin being confessed only to God for it was He alone whom man had offended. David, in the Old Testament, said to God: ***"Against You alone have I sinned..."*** (Psalm 51:6; cf.Luke 15:18).

Auricular confession is nowhere to be found in the writings of **Augustine, Origen, Nestorius, Tertullian, Jerome, Chrysostom or Athanasius**. All of these early 'Church fathers' wrote volumes that dealt with the practice and duties of Christians, and yet not once did they ever speak of the need of confessing one's sins to a priest! Now, these facts cannot be denied— they are not up for discussion—**they cannot be**

challenged, and therefore must not be ignored! Will you, the Roman Catholic, continue to follow the mere inventions of men, or will you turn to the Word of God and adhere to sound and reliable teaching?

In the early Church *"there were, to be sure, public confessions before local church groups, in order that offenders might be restored to fellowship....such confessions were open, general and voluntary, and were as different from auricular confession as light is from darkness."*[12]

"To those who value the testimony of primitive Christianity the fact that this practice (of confession to a priest) *is not to be found during the earliest centuries of the Christian Church should demonstrate conclusively the vanity and needlessness of the entire concept."*[13]

In later years, as the Roman Catholic Church became more powerful, the confessional was introduced for those seeking counsel and advice from the priest. At the outset, auricular confession was on a voluntary basis and was introduced into the Roman Church in the 5th century by Pope Leo the Great. Yet not until the 4th Lateran Council in 1215 A.D., under Pope Innocent I, was it made compulsory, requiring all Roman Catholics to confess and seek absolution from a priest at least once a year! It is interesting to note that it was during this 13th century that priestly and papal power was greatly extended. Needless to say, this is far from a mere coincidence.

As will be borne out in a later chapter, the only 'priest' mentioned in the New Testament in relation to the Christian Faith, is Jesus Christ. If, then, there is no such thing as a 'Christian priest' apart from Christ Jesus Himself, auricular confession should therefore be poured into His ear and not that of the Roman Catholic priest.

THE POWER OF THE CONFESSIONAL

As was the case with the priests of old Babylon, so it is today for the modern priest of Rome. The confessional is a means of great power over the people and a way of acquiring knowledge (secrets) from individual families to governments.

Through the confessional, Roman Catholic priests are made privy, not only to the sins and secrets of individuals and their families—which often include the detailed sexual problems occurring between husbands and wives—but they are also made familiar, by the agency of the confessional, with the sins and secrets of presidents and prime ministers, even kings. The confessor of the king of France often boasted: *"With my God in my hand (referring to the communion wafer), and my king at my knee (referring to the confessional) who can greater be?"*

"What greater intellectual and moral bondage for human beings could be imagined, or what more dangerous power could be possessed, than that of the Roman (Catholic) confessional? History furnishes many impressive warnings; such

as Charles IX and the massacre of St. Bartholomew; or of Louis XIV and the cruel revocation of the Edict of Nantes, 1685."[14]

Former Roman Catholic priest, **Lucien Vinet**, who himself heard countless confessions and who knows firsthand how the Roman Catholic system works, has this to say about auricular confession: *"It has been instituted, we priests know it so well, primarily to make it possible for the agents of Rome to control the most intimate reactions of human hearts and minds in the interests of the authority and prestige of a human political and religious system."* **Vinet** adds: *"When an organization such as the Roman system can control not only the education, the family and policies of the civil government of its members, but even their very thoughts and desires, we do not wonder that it can prosper and succeed. Roman Catholics, whether they feel that they ought to admit it or not, are forced into submission to Romanism through the process of torturing auricular confession."*[15]

ROMAN CATHOLIC 'PROOF' OF AURICULAR CONFESSION

There are two main Scriptures to which the Roman Catholic Church refers in defence of its *'confession to a priest'* doctrine: John 20:23 and James 5:16. As we saw at the outset of this booklet, one Roman Catholic Catechism states that *"Sins are forgiven by the power of God, which Jesus Christ has given to the priests of His church."*

Though the Roman Catholic Church freely admits that ultimately it is God ALONE who can forgive sins, she insists that He does so through the Roman Catholic priest. John 20:23 is the principal verse used to enforce this claim. Article 198 of the Roman Catechism states: *"Jesus Christ gave to the priests of His Church the power of forgiving sins..."* The article later quotes the Words of the Lord Jesus spoken to His disciples in John 20:23: ***"Whose sins you forgive are forgiven them, and whose sins you retain are retained."*** The footnotes to this verse in the Roman Catholic New American Bible inform us that *"The Council of Trent defined that this power to forgive sins is exercised in the sacrament of penance."*

This verse from the Gospel of John is interpreted to mean that it is the prerogative of the priest to forgive sins or to hold back forgiveness. In contrast to this, the Lord Jesus makes it perfectly clear in Mark 3:28,29 that ***"...all sins and all blasphemies that people utter WILL BE FORGIVEN THEM. But whoever blasphemes against the Holy Spirit will never have forgiveness...."*** The book, *'The Catholic Religion'*, agrees and declares that *"No matter how serious a sin is, God will forgive it if the sinner is truly sorry and asks pardon."*[16]

However, in commenting on the priest's 'power' to grant and refuse forgiveness, *'The Catholic Encyclopedia'* states that *"In order for him to do this, sins 'specifically and in detail' (according to the Council of Trent), must be confessed to him, for, 'How can a wise and prudent judgement be rendered if the priest be in ignorance of the cause on which judgement is pronounced? And how can he obtain the requisite knowledge unless it come from the spontaneous acknowledgement of the sinner?' Having given priests the authority to forgive sins, it is inconsistent to believe, says the article, 'that Christ had intended to provide some other means of forgiveness such as confessing to God alone.' Confession to a priest for those who commit sins after their baptism, is 'necessary unto salvation.'"*[17]

What is in fact inconsistent and totally unbiblical is a sinful man approaching a priest—another sinful man—for the forgiveness of sins committed against God, when, as will be detailed later, the true Christian has direct access to God through the Lord Jesus Christ!! Not to mention the fact, which the Roman Catholic Bible clearly states, ***"...WHO BUT GOD ALONE CAN FORGIVE SINS?"*** (Luke 5:21).

Furthermore, to teach that confession to a priest is *'necessary unto salvation'* would mean that for the first 1,000 years of Christianity no one attained salvation, for the concept of confession to a priest had not even been heard of!! The whole system is utter nonsense.

Let it be known that the Roman Catholic Bible does not contain **any** examples of **any** apostle saying to **anyone**, *'I absolve you from your sin,'* or even, *'your sins are forgiven you'*. If this power to forgive sin was delegated to the apostles by Jesus, as is the contention of Roman Catholicism, they undoubtedly would have called attention to such a vital doctrine in their writings; or at the very least there could be found a place where such power to forgive sins was displayed. Yet the Roman Catholic Bible contains no such evidence. Only the one true God, can and does forgive sin. Psalm 130:4 states: ***"...with YOU is forgiveness and so YOU are revered"*** (cf. Psalm 32:5; Daniel 9:9).

Notice, too, that John 20 does not say that Jesus spoke to His *priests*, but to His *disciples* (v.20). The only Christian priesthood mentioned in the New Testament is the priesthood of believers. The apostle John, writing to the seven churches in Asia, said: ***"...To Him who loves us and has freed us from our sins by His blood, who has made us into a kingdom, PRIESTS FOR HIS GOD AND FATHER, TO HIM BE GLORY AND POWER FOREVER (AND EVER). AMEN"*** (Revelation 1:5,6).

The Roman Catholic Bible says that all true believers in Christ Jesus are to allow themselves to be ***"...built into a spiritual house to be a HOLY PRIESTHOOD..."*** (1 Peter 2:5). In verse 9 of the same chapter, Peter says to believers, ***"...you are a chosen race, A ROYAL PRIESTHOOD..."*** (cf. Revelation 5:10; 20:6). The entire Body of Christ, which is made up of all true believers, is a priesthood. It is not something that is exclusive to a small group of men.

What the expressions in John 20:23 do indicate is the fact that the disciples were given

The Lord Jesus Christ states, in Luke 24:47, that it is written: ***"...repentance, for the forgiveness of sins would be preached in His name to all the nations..."*** On no occasion did the apostles forgive anyone of their sin, for they could not. They did, however, by the preaching of the Gospel, **proclaim** the forgiveness of sins. They were, as is every true Christian today, to **declare** the forgiveness of sins through the preaching of the Gospel.

The other Scripture cited by the Roman Catholic Church as confirming the doctrine of auricular confession is James 5:16: ***"Therefore, confess your sins to one another, and pray for one another that you may be healed..."*** This Scripture, taken from the passage in James 5:13-16, deals with the anointing of the sick and the forgiveness of any sins which may have caused the sickness. Primarily, James is here prescribing confession and prayer to those who were sick, for he adds in v.16 ***"...that you may be healed..."*** *"The duty inculcated, and which is equally binding on all now, is, that if we are sick,* *and are conscious that we have injured any persons, (we are) to make confession to <u>them</u>.*"[19] **Not to a priest!**

James tells believers to *"...confess your sins TO ONE ANOTHER..."* (v.16). He evidently is not talking about confessing their sins to a priest in order to obtain absolution, but is telling them that they are to confess sin, which has been committed against another, to that one **whom they have sinned against**, and that those who have sinned against us should come to us and ask forgiveness and not to a third party, such as a priest.

In Matthew 5:23,24, Jesus instructs believers that, upon recollection of their having grieved a brother by sinning against him, they are to go and *"...be reconciled with your brother..."* Jesus Christ does not tell His people to confess their sin to a priest, but to seek out the offended brother and confess their sin to him.

A key phrase in James 5:16 is: *"...to one another..."* James is saying that they should CONFESS THEIR SINS TO EACH OTHER!! In his letter to the Ephesians, Paul encourages them to be *"...FORGIVING ONE ANOTHER as God has forgiven you in Christ"* (4:32); and in Colossians 3:13, Paul's instruction is: *"bearing with one another and FORGIVING ONE ANOTHER, if one has a grievance against another..."*

In addition, the confession specified in James 5:16 does not refer to a person in health that he might be saved, but to a person in sickness that he might be healed. Moreover, there is no mention of a priest or any minister in this verse!

CONFESSION TO WHOM? - WHAT DOES THE ROMAN CATHOLIC BIBLE SAY?

The Roman Catholic Church teaches that we <u>must</u> confess our sins to a priest in order that we may be forgiven. In fact, she goes so far as to say that *"...it is necessary by <u>divine law</u> to confess to a priest each and every mortal sin..."*[20] Roman Catholicism declares that salvation itself depends on this.

But just exactly where did this *'divine law'* come from we may well ask? **It certainly did not come from God.** Nor indeed can it be found in the pages of the Roman Catholic Bible! The 'Church fathers' knew nothing of its existence. Never once is there any mention of a priest—in connection with the Christian Faith—in the entire New Testament. In actual fact, there is no mention of the office of a priest in all the listings of Offices and Officers that were to be appointed in the Christian Church, for the simple reason that true Christianity has only ONE priest and He is the GREAT HIGH PRIEST, JESUS CHRIST!

While we are on the subject of priests, allow me to add something that should be most revealing to you, the Roman Catholic—the primary function of a priest is to perform sacrifices. The Roman Catholic Bible informs us that there has been ONE sacrifice performed ONCE AND FOR ALL, that of the Lamb of God, Jesus Christ. Some

Scriptures from the Letter to the Hebrews will bear this out:

Hebrews 9:26 - ***"...But now ONCE FOR ALL He has appeared at the end of the ages to take away sin by HIS SACRIFICE."***

Hebrews 9:28 - ***"...so also Christ, offered ONCE to take away the sins of many..."***

Hebrews 10:14 - ***"For by ONE OFFERING He has made perfect forever those who are being consecrated."***

Hebrews 10:18 - ***"Where there is forgiveness of these (sins), there is NO LONGER OFFERING FOR SIN."***

Seeing as there has been ONE sacrifice made for all time, there are no supplementary sacrifices required and therefore no further need for priests! The Roman Catholic Bible itself supports this fact in its lists of Church officers: ***"...apostles...prophets...teachers..."*** (1 Corinthians 12:28); and in Ephesians 4:11: ***"...apostles... prophets... evangelists... pastors and teachers."*** Again, no reference to priests.

It is quite obvious from the pages of the Roman Catholic Bible whom the true believer is to confess his sins to and whom he is to seek forgiveness from. In the Gospel of Mark 2:7, the Jews asked the question, ***"...who but GOD ALONE can forgive sins?"*** The Jewish priesthood of the Old Testament did on no occasion hear the confession of each individual's sins; nor did they ever give absolution, for they knew this power belonged to God, and that God alone was the One who could, and did, forgive sins, and that He appoints this power to no man!

We see from Acts 8:22 that the apostle Peter, whom Rome contends was the first Pope, did not hear Simon the Samarian's confession. Simon did not confess his sins to Peter but was directed by the apostle to: ***"Repent of this wickedness of yours and PRAY TO THE LORD that, if possible, your intention may be forgiven."*** If ever there was an opportunity for Peter to display his alleged 'power to forgive', this was it. Yet we see that Peter did not dare take on the role that belongs to GOD ALONE!

True repentance, which is a gift given by God to the sinner, will always lead one to the true God; to an acknowledgement of, and a turning away from, one's sins and to a wholehearted belief in God's only Gospel. Judas, the traitor, who of course did not go to God—the only One who can make us clean from sin and guilt—was so overcome with guilt that he committed suicide. The sorrow he had for his sin was a worldly sorrow which leads to death. There is a godly sorrow which leads one to God and eternal life (see 2 Corinthians 7:9,10). It is to God, and God alone, whom the Roman Catholic Bible directs the believer to confess his sins: ***"If we acknowledge our sins, He is faithful and just and will forgive our sins and cleanse us from every***

wrongdoing" (1 John 1:9). The prophet Micah says: **"Who is there like You, the God who removes guilt and pardons sin..."** (7:18).

Further evidence from the pages of the Roman Catholic Bible of just who people turned to when in need of forgiveness may be found in Luke 18:9-14. This passage describes for us the parable of the tax collector and the Pharisee. The Pharisee thanked God that he was not a sinner as the publican, and no doubt those like him. But the tax collector came humbly to God, **"...beat his breast and prayed, 'O God, be merciful to me a sinner'"** (v.13). This man did not need a priest, he did not seek a priest, but went directly to God confessing the fact that he was a sinner, and Jesus said in verse 14 that *this* man **"...went home justified..."**

The Roman Catholic Bible proclaims that all true believers may **"...confidently approach the throne of grace to receive mercy and to find grace for timely help"** (Hebrews 4:16). All true believers have **"...through the blood of Jesus...confidence of entrance into the Sanctuary"** (Hebrews 10:19), **"for through Him we both have access in one Spirit to the Father"** (Ephesians 2:18; cf.3:12; Romans 5:2). These Scriptures demonstrate clearly that every Gospel-believing Christian has **DIRECT ACCESS TO GOD** and needs no intermediary other than the Great High Priest, Jesus Christ.

The apostle John, writing to the believers, declared: **"...if anyone does sin, we have an Advocate with the Father, JESUS CHRIST THE**

RIGHTEOUS ONE" (1 John 2:1). The Lord Jesus Christ is the believer's sole Advocate with the Father. He has not given this role to, nor does He share it with, any priest of the Roman Catholic Church.

It is important to note that not every Roman Catholic priest who enters the confessional is convinced that he has the 'power to forgive'. One former priest of Rome, **Dr. Joseph Zacchello**, had many misgivings. His following admission no doubt speaks for many: _"Where my doubts were really troubling me was inside the confessional box. People were coming to me, kneeling down in front of me, confessing their sins to me. And I, with a sign of the cross, was promising that I had the power to forgive their sins. I, a sinner, a man, was taking God's place, God's right, and that terrible voice was penetrating me saying, 'You are depriving God of His glory; If sinners want to obtain forgiveness of their sins they must go to God and not to you; It is God's law that they have broken, not yours. To God, therefore, they must make confession; and to God alone they must pray for forgiveness. No man can forgive sins, but Jesus can and does forgive sins.'"[21]_

To the thinking Roman Catholic, I ask this question: _'Why go to a human priest, a sinful man, to seek forgiveness which he cannot give, when the Word of God clearly directs and instructs His people to go to the GREAT HIGH PRIEST, to the SINLESS MAN, the Lord Jesus Christ?!!'_

CHRIST JESUS - THE ONLY MEDIATOR BETWEEN GOD AND MAN!!

As was established earlier, the Roman Catholic Bible teaches that there is only ONE Mediator between God and man, and He is the Lord Jesus Christ. The New Testament knows nothing of priests acting as intermediaries between God and man, nor incidentally, does it give the role of Mediator or co-mediator to Mary! Paul's first letter to Timothy plainly states: ***"For there is one God. There is also ONE MEDIATOR between God and the human race, CHRIST JESUS..."*** (1 Timothy 2:5).

With the Son of God as our Mediator, what need have we for any other? *"To interpose any official body of men between the individual Christian and God is to run counter to the very genius of the Christian religion."*[22]

The only way a man can find peace with God and be forgiven of all his sins, past, present and future, is to come to Him, not through a human priest, but through the Lord Jesus Christ. The following two Scriptures from the Roman Catholic Bible should dispense, for all time, any doubt of this:

Hebrews 4:14 - ***"...WE HAVE A GREAT HIGH PRIEST who has passed through the heavens, JESUS, THE SON OF GOD..."***

Hebrews 7:25 - ***"...He*** (Jesus) ***is always able to save those who APPROACH GOD THROUGH***

__HIM, since He lives forever to make intercession for them"__

<u>IN CONCLUSION...</u>

From the above information and Scriptures, we may confidently say that True confession, as taught in the pages of the Roman Catholic Bible, is when it is made **directly to God in the name of the Lord Jesus Christ.** Though the Roman Catholic Church claims certain Scriptures in support of their doctrine of confession to a priest, we have seen that this teaching does not concur with other passages from the Roman Catholic Bible. They are texts that have been taken out of their context and given meanings that were never intended by the writers, and which support a practice that is pagan in its origin, and therefore could not be of God.

The Christian's Advocate with the Father is not a common man, it is not a sinful human priest. The believer's one and only Advocate is the sinless Son of the Living God, the One who died for God's elect and rose again that they too might live—the Lord Jesus Christ. With directions as clear as we have from the Roman Catholic Bible, why would any man insist on confessing his sins to another man, when he has been given clear directions in Scripture to go directly to God and confess his sins?

The confessional is a place that is often feared and approached with apprehension by some. To others it is a place of extreme embarrassment, especially Roman Catholic women, who are at times subjected to very personal questions that often deal with intimate details of their married life. **Lucien Vinet**, a former Roman Catholic priest, expresses his concern and compassion toward these women: *"Poor Roman Catholic women! We know well that your kind souls are tortured to death by this terrible Roman obligation of telling, not only your sins, but also the most intimate secrets of your married life. As an ex-priest I can tell you that these mental tortures imposed upon your souls are not a prescription of the Saviour of mankind to obtain forgiveness of your sins, but are pure inventions of men to keep your minds and hearts under the control of a system, the torturous Roman religious organization. I must admit that as a priest I had no power to forgive your sins. No priest has such powers."*[23]

Confession to a priest provides the Roman Catholic with a false sense of security, a belief that all is right with he and his god. Sin needs to be confessed/acknowledged to the Holy God, through His Son Jesus Christ, for it is He whom we have offended! Repentance also needs to take place, for the Lord Jesus said: ***"...Repent and believe in the Gospel"*** (Mark 1:15) and ***"...if you do not repent you will all perish..."*** (Luke 13:3). Proverbs 28:13 declares: ***"He who conceals his sin prospers not, but he who CONFESSES AND FORSAKES them obtains mercy."***

If people would only believe the Gospel. *"If people would only read their Bibles,* *and believe what God tells them, they would soon find by happy experience the power of His truth, and be incapable of accepting those deadly errors which are ensnaring and enslaving so many in these days, of which private confession and priestly absolution are the most pernicious.*"[24]

Perhaps the most fitting way to close our study on confession is to allow the words of another former Roman Catholic priest, **Charles Chiniquy**, to speak to the heart of you, the Roman Catholic: *"With a blush on my face, and regret in my heart, I confess before God and man, that I have been through the confessional plunged for twenty-five years in that bottomless sea of iniquity, in which the blind priests of Rome have to swim day and night....Yes I was bound in conscience, to put into the ears, the mind, the imagination, the memory, the heart and soul of women and girls, questions of such a nature, the direct and immediate tendency of which is to fill the minds and hearts of both priests and penitents with thoughts and temptations of such a degrading nature, that I do not know any words adequate to express them. Pagan antiquity has never seen any institution more polluting than the confessional. I was degraded and polluted by the confessional just as all the priests of Rome are. It has required the whole blood of the great Victim, who died on Calvary for sinners, to purify me.*"[25]

Dear Roman Catholic, repent and believe the Gospel of Christ and His Righteousness and confess your sins to God through Jesus Christ alone. He awaits all His chosen ones with eyes of mercy and a heart of grace.

COME OUT FROM HER....

The purpose of this booklet has not been to judge or condemn you, the Roman Catholic, but has been designed to educate you, to inform you of facts and proper biblical teaching which the Roman Catholic Church has not given you. It has been written in order to provide you with historical facts about the origins of many of your Church's teachings and traditions. **You have read for yourself what the Roman Catholic Church admits to and what your own Roman Catholic Bible says, and doesn't say—what it teaches and simply does not support.** Ultimately, this booklet is a plea for you to come out of the Roman Catholic Church, away from all its man-made doctrines and pagan practices, away from its false gospel. **God must be worshipped HIS way, for no other way is acceptable unto Him.** There is no other way to worship the true God—**and therefore be a saved, justified and true follower of God**—other than the way He has prescribed in His Holy Word. **There is no Gospel that must be believed, by which a man is saved, other than the one that reveals the Righteousness of Christ.**

We have presented the truth to you. **Verifiable truth.** We have quoted from many sources approved by your own Church including a Church approved Bible. But do not believe things simply because you saw them written in a booklet. The Bible commends those who properly investigate what is presented to them as truth and we encourage you to do so. In Acts 17:11 the apostle Paul and Silas preached to the people at Berea. The Roman Catholic Bible says that ***"These...were more fair-minded than those in Thessalonica, for they received the word with all willingness and EXAMINED THE SCRIPTURES DAILY TO DETERMINE WHETHER THESE THINGS WERE SO."*** The Scriptures were their sole authority. They did not refer to the writings of mere men, seeking out their opinions, but went immediately to the Holy Word of God **knowing** that His Word alone could be trusted, and was the sure test for all teachings being presented as God's own decrees (see 2 Peter 1:19). Paul and Silas were not offended by their examining and putting to the test what they was saying, they did not say *'How dare you examine what we have said to you; don't you know who we are?'* **Every Christian, indeed every person, is to examine by the Holy Scriptures all that is presented to him as God's teaching, and if it does not match with the Scriptures, you can be sure it did not come from God and is to be rejected out of hand.** Writing to true believers, John said, ***"Beloved, DO NOT TRUST every spirit BUT TEST the spirits to see whether they belong to God, because many false prophets have gone out into the world"*** (1 John 4:1).

The subtle deceptiveness of the Roman Catholic Church is that she teaches some truths of Scripture but always adds to them, something which the Scriptures roundly condemn: ***"Add NOTHING to HIS Words, lest He reprove you, and you be exposed as a deceiver"*** (Proverbs 30:6). In speaking against such deception the Lord Jesus warned His disciples to ***"...Look out, and beware of the leaven of the Pharisees and Sadducees"*** (Matthew 16:6 cf. Galatians 5:9). Later, the disciples ***"...understood that He was not telling them to beware of the leaven of bread, but of THE TEACHING of the Pharisees and Sadducees"*** (Matthew 16:12). The Pharisees and Sadducees were the religious leaders in Jesus' day.The apostle Paul warned: ***"...watch out for those who create dissensions and obstacles, in opposition to the teaching that you learned; avoid them. For such people do not serve our Lord Christ but their own appetites, and by fair and flattering speech they deceive the hearts of the innocent"*** (Romans 16:17,18). EXAMINE EVERYTHING! TEST EVERYTHING BY THE WORD OF GOD! **For we are dealing with eternal issues here. We are dealing with heaven and hell, and what a person believes determines their eternal destiny, for the doctrine you hold to is the surest evidence of whether or not it is the true God Who has revealed Himself to you or whether it is a false god whom you have embraced.**

Some examples of such deceptiveness are as follows: the Roman Catholic Church teaches her followers to pray the Lord's prayer, but they are encouraged to do so whilst holding the Rosary which is a pagan invention and has nothing to do with true Christianity. Yes, Rome agrees that God alone forgives sin, but they add that this power to forgive has been given to her priests and one must go *to them* to receive it and not directly to God the Father through Jesus His Son, as the Scriptures prescribe. Yes, Roman Catholicism teaches that the Bible is the Word of God but it considers tradition to be *equal* to God's precious Holy Word and insists that she is the only true interpreter of Scripture! **In other words, what ROME says God's Word is saying is what is to be obeyed, rather than what the Scripture's interpretation of Itself is saying! Compare Scripture with Scripture, not Scripture with a man's interpretation.** All along, Roman Catholicism adds to God's Word and in other instances withholds certain parts of it, such as the second Commandment, from its publications. It is true that Roman Catholicism teaches 'the death, burial and resurrection' of Jesus Christ but it is vitally important to note that while she may correctly teach some aspects of these things—things which are aligned with historical fact—the Roman Catholic Church **does not** teach the death, burial and resurrection of Jesus Christ ***"...in accordance with the Scriptures..."*** (1 Corinthians 15:3,4).

It is no accident that so much pagan tradition is found today in Roman Catholicism. It has been carefully managed and seen to, that old pagan/occultic rites and traditions, which the Bible calls demonic, are continued to be adhered to and promoted as vigilantly as they were by the early pagans, but now with a Christian veneer thus setting up the Roman Catholic Church as the unmistakably identifiable anti-christian system referred to as 'Babylon' in the Bible. Roman Catholicism stands today not only against Christ, for it does not teach His Gospel, but Rome has also, in a most vulgar way, usurped Christ's position. The papacy claims that **it** is the vicar of Christ on earth, rather than the Holy Spirit as the Word of God says.

That which immediately reveals a religious organization's ungodly foundation may be seen in the gospel it teaches. What a person, or organization such as the Roman Catholic Church, says about **Who Jesus Christ is, what He has done and for whom He has done it**—in other words His Person and His Work—will reveal whether or not that person or organization is of God (see 2 John 9). After having preached to them the True and only Gospel of salvation which reveals the true God and true Christ, Paul the apostle warned the believers in Galatia that ***"...even if we or an angel from heaven should preach to you a gospel OTHER THAN the one that we preached to you, let that one be accursed"*** (Galatians 1:8).

There are many who by nature are religious; many who are extremely zealous for what they believe to be the things of God, yet Scripture reminds us that by nature ***"There is no one just, not one, there is no one who understands, there is no one who seeks God"*** (Romans 3:10,11). Saving, God-given faith in the true and only Gospel of God shows that it is the true God Who has revealed Himself. **Belief in any gospel other than that one and only Gospel of God reveals that it is not the true God Who has revealed Himself but rather a false god who cannot save.**

We implore you to come out of the Roman Catholic Church. A Church which is headed, not by the Lord Jesus Christ, for it does not promote His Gospel, but by a man who calls himself the 'Pope', and who allows himself to be addressed as 'Holy Father', a title which God **ALONE** is worthy. God ALONE is Father, and God ALONE is Holy. The Lord Jesus only ever referred to God as 'Father', and in Revelation 15:4 Jesus, praying to the Father said: ***"...You ALONE are Holy..."*** How dare ANY man take upon himself a title of which ONLY God is worthy! Not incidentally, the Lord Jesus Christ also said to His followers not to call any man on earth father, that is in a spiritual sense, for One was their Father and He resides in heaven: ***"Call no one on earth your father; you have but one Father in heaven"*** (Matthew 23:9). Roman Catholicism responds to these words of the Lord Jesus by calling *every one of its priests 'father'*, and demanding that everyone else, Roman

Catholic or not, do likewise despite admitting in their footnotes to Matthew 23:9 that, *"...Jesus forbids not only the titles (rabbi, father and master) but the spirit of superiority and pride that is shown by their acceptance."*

Pope Leo XIII once blasphemously declared: *"The Pope holds upon this earth the place of God Almighty..."* **Robert Bellermine**, famous Jesuit Cardinal of the 16th century and also a saint of the Roman Catholic Church, had this to say: *"All the names which in the Scriptures are applied to Christ by virtue of which it is established that He is over the Church, all the same names are applied to the Pope."* The *Catholique Nationale* of Paris, in its July 13, 1895 issue, contained the following claim made by the then archbishop of Venice, later to become Pope Pius X. He said, *"The Pope is not only the representative of Jesus Christ, but he is Jesus Christ Himself hidden under the veil of the flesh..."* Dear Roman Catholic, **the Pope is NOT Jesus Christ! JESUS CHRIST IS GOD!! ONLY through the Lord Jesus Christ is there salvation, not through the Pope and his 'church' of Rome.**

"History is replete with sayings that mocked Romanism's false claim to celibacy: 'The holiest hermit has his whore'" and *"'Rome has more prostitutes than any other city because she has the most celibates'"* are examples. Pope Pius II called Rome *'The only city run by bastards, the sons and grandsons of popes and cardinals'.*

"Even Roman Catholic historians admit that among the popes were some of the most degenerate and unconscionable ogres in all history. More than one pope was slain by a husband who found him in bed with his wife. To call such a man 'His holiness vicar of Christ' makes a mockery of holiness and Christ. Yet the name of each of these mass murderers, fornicators, robbers, warmongers—some guilty of the massacre of thousands—is emblazoned in honor on the Church's official list of Peter's alleged successors, the popes" ('The Berean Call', July '94, p.2).

"Will you believe the words of the Roman Catholic Church or will you believe the words of the Roman Catholic Bible? It is for you to decide. Remember, there are only two religions in the entire world, man's and God's. If it is not the truth of God that you are believing, then you have embraced the lies of the Devil." **You have embraced a false gospel wherein is no salvation.** *"Man's religion is by works—his own efforts, his fastings and prayers, his obedience to the Church. That, in effect, makes him his own saviour. God's is by faith in the finished work of Jesus Christ. Jesus paid it all... The Roman Catholic Bible states clearly: **"...we have been JUSTIFIED BY FAITH, we have peace with God through our Lord Jesus Christ...**Romans 5:1."* The Roman Catholic Bible makes it perfectly clear that man cannot save himself and that Christ is his only hope; his only Saviour."*[26]

"Salvation is not dependent on a human priest, Mary, Baptism, the saints, the sacraments, the Mass, confession, good works, membership in the Roman Catholic Church or the Pope."

Salvation is not gained by our loyalty or service to a person—**be they our parents or grandparents and their religious traditions which they have passed down to us**—or to an institution such as the Roman Catholic Church, but rather by our **acceptance of the truth**!! *Jesus said: **"...I am the Way and the Truth and the Life. No one comes to the Father EXCEPT THROUGH ME"** (John 14:6) and **"I am the Gate. Whoever enters through Me will be saved..."*** (John 10:9). *Acts 4:12 says:* **'There is NO salvation through ANYONE else, nor is there ANY other name under heaven given to the human race by which we are to be saved.'**

It matters not how religious a person is or how sincere he might be in his religious pursuits, if a man has not the Gospel of God, if he does not **"...remain in the teaching of the Christ** (he) **does not have God..."** (2 John 9). **"That all who have not believed the truth but have approved wrongdoing may be condemned"** (2 Thessalonians 2:12). Scripture also speaks of the vengeance that will be had upon the enemies of God **"...at the revelation of the Lord Jesus from heaven with His mighty angels, in blazing fire, inflicting punishment on those who do not acknowledge God and on those WHO DO NOT OBEY THE GOSPEL of our Lord Jesus. These will pay the penalty of eternal** *ruin, separated from the presence of the Lord and from the glory of His power"* (1 Thessalonians 7-9).

Only through the Gospel of Christ wherein is revealed the Righteousness of Christ, without which no man can be saved, is there true salvation: ***"For I am not ashamed of the Gospel. IT IS THE POWER OF GOD for the salvation of everyone who believes: for the Jew first, and then Greek. For in it is revealed the Righteousness of God from faith to faith; as it is written, the one who is righteous <u>by faith</u> will live"*** (Romans 1:16,17). Central to the Gospel message is the Person and Work of Jesus Christ and, according to the Scriptures, if one is wrong about Christ, if one has embraced erroneous doctrine concerning Christ the Person and His Work, one is not merely in need of correction yet nevertheless saved, one has in fact fallen for another jesus who is identified by false doctrine, and thus remains in a lost state. **Only in the True Jesus is their salvation. Belief, however sincere, in a false jesus CANNOT SAVE!** You see, not only does the apostle Paul state that the Gospel is the power of God but he also defines this statement in 1 Corinthians 1:18: ***"THE MESSAGE OF THE CROSS is foolishness to those who are perishing, but to us who are being saved IT*** (THE CROSS) ***IS THE POWER OF GOD."***

Belief in false doctrines concerning Christ constitutes a belief in *another* gospel, one which does not represent the true Christ

but a false savior (see 2 Corinthians 11:3,4). The Holy Spirit is the Spirit of Truth (John 14:17; 15:26; 16:13) and never presents a man with, nor leads him to believe, a false gospel: ***"But when He comes, the Spirit of Truth, He will guide you to all truth..."*** (John 16:13). Jesus prayed, ***"Consecrate them in the Truth. Your Word is Truth"*** (John 17:17). The true believer is consecrated, or sanctified, through the truth which is the Word of God and not through the lies of men. Speaking to saved men, the apostle Paul stated: ***"...God chose you as the firstfruits for salvation through sanctification BY THE SPIRIT AND BELIEF IN TRUTH"*** (2 Thessalonians 2:13). There is no true sanctification if one's faith is not in the Truth of God.

Only by belief in Christ's Gospel, which says that man is dead in sin, without God and without hope of salvation by anything he is or does in an effort to please God and gain His favor, is a man saved: ***"Therefore, remember that at one time you...were at that time without Christ...without hope and without God in the world"*** (Ephesians 2:11-13). ***"You were dead in your transgressions and sins"*** (Ephesians 2:1). ***"All have sinned and are deprived of the glory of God"*** (Romans 3:23).

Only by belief in Christ's Gospel, which says that a man is saved not by works, not by anything he has done, is doing or will do, but solely by the grace and mercy of God, is a man saved: ***"...a person is not justified by works***

of the law but through faith in Jesus Christ, even we have believed in Christ Jesus that we may be justified by faith in Christ and not by works of the law, because by works of the law no one will be justified" (Galatians 1:16). The cry of the truly justified sinner is that he is *"...justified freely by His grace through the redemption in Christ Jesus, Whom God set forth as an expiation, through faith, by His blood..."* (Romans 3:24,25).

Only by belief in Christ's Gospel, which says a man is not saved based on anything he has done but solely by the grace of God through the election of grace, is a man saved: *"...God chose you as the firstfruits for salvation through sanctification by the Spirit and belief in truth"* (2 Thessalonians 2:13). *"As He chose us in Him, before the foundation of the world, to be holy and without blemish before Him"* (Ephesians 1:4); *"He saved us and called us to a holy life, NOT ACCORDING TO OUR WORKS, but according to His own design and the grace bestowed on us in Christ Jesus before time began"* (2 Timothy 1:9). No saved person ever came to God first (see 1 John 4:19). In every case God came to the person first and gave them the gift of salvation, not because they had in any way earned this gift, but freely and only by the will of God and the grace of God. Scripture says that by nature *"...there is no one who seeks God"* (Romans 3:11). *"But when one does not work, yet believes in the One Who justifies the ungodly, his faith is credited as* *righteousness. So also David declares the blessedness of the person to whom God credits righteousness apart from works"* (Romans 4:5,6).

Only by belief in Christ's Gospel, which says that Christ died exclusively for His people, those whom God had given Him (see John 17:2), and has provided them with an atonement for their sin, having their sins imputed, or charged, to Him and imputing unto them His perfect righteousness, is a man saved. Jesus said: *"I am the good shepherd. A good shepherd lays down His life for the sheep....I will lay down My life for the sheep"* (John 10:11,15). Writing to true believers Paul said, *"For our sake He made Him to be sin* (for us) *who did not know sin, so that we might become the righteousness of God in Him"* (2 Corinthians 5:21).

Only by belief in Christ's Gospel, which says that all His people shall come to Him, hear and believe His Gospel, is there true salvation. None whom the Lord has given unto Him shall perish, none shall be plucked from His Hand, but all for whom He died shall be saved: *"My sheep hear My voice; I know them, and they follow Me. I give them eternal life, and they shall never perish. No one can take them out of My hand"* (John 10:27,28). *"Everything that the Father gives Me WILL come to Me..."* (John 6:37).

Only by belief in Christ's Gospel, which states that none for whom He died shall ever perish, but all who have had their sins charged to Him shall be given eternal life, is a man saved. Salvation has not only been *obtained* for God's chosen, but it is eternally *maintained* by the Will of God and all that Christ has done: ***"...Give glory to Your Son, so that Your Son may glorify You, just as You gave Him authority over all people, so that He may give eternal life to all You gave Him"*** (John 17:1,2). Christ has not only obtained salvation for His people, by paying the penalty for their sin and imputing to them His righteousness, He also maintains their salvation by His eternal and completed work upon the cross. Thus ALL the glory for salvation belongs to God and none of it is shared with any man based on his works. **Only THIS Gospel gives ALL the glory to God for salvation and wherein there is no room for man to boast in anything he is or has done.**

Only by belief in Christ's Gospel, which states that no man is, or can be saved by his own righteousness, by his own efforts at obedience to God's Law, but only by the perfect Righteousness of Jesus Christ which is freely imputed based on His grace and mercy ALONE to all those for whom He died, is a man saved. The apostle Paul wanted to ***"...be found in Him, not having any righteousness of my own based on the law but that which comes through faith in Christ, the righteousness from God, depending on faith..."*** (Philippians 3:9). Paul considered all that he was and did in the realm of religion as rubbish, **and therefore himself as a lost person,** before knowing Christ and His Gospel: ***"...because of the supreme good of knowing Christ Jesus my Lord. For His sake I have accepted the loss of all things and I consider them so much rubbish..."*** (Philippians 3:8).

Only those who have heard the Word of Truth, God's Mighty Gospel, can be said to truly hope in the true Christ: ***"In Him you also, who have heard the word of truth, THE GOSPEL OF YOUR SALVATION, and have believed in Him, were sealed with the promised Holy Spirit"*** (Ephesians 1:13).

Look then to the only true Jesus Who is the Author and Finisher of the Faith which God gives and which only believes in the true Gospel.

ANY AND ALL FAITH IN ANOTHER JESUS WILL NOT SAVE.

ANY AND ALL FAITH IN ANOTHER GOSPEL WILL NOT SAVE.

"Whoever believes (THE Gospel) ***and is baptized will be saved; whoever does not believe will be condemned"*** (Mark 16:16).

The true born again believer knows that ***"...by grace you have been saved through faith, and this is not from you; it is the gift of God; it is not from works, so no one may boast"*** (Ephesians 2:8,9).

May God bless each and every one of you with His Truth as revealed in His Gospel.

<u>NOTES</u>

[1] The Baltimore Catechism, p.315.

[2] Roman Catholic Catechism, p.50, article 197, 1937, Australian Catholic Truth Society.

[3] Roman Catholicism, L. Boettner, p.203, 1962, Presbyterian & Reformed Publishing Company.

[4] The Catholic Religion, p.135, Imprimatur, E. McAuliffe, Catholic Enquiry Centre, 1966.
[5] The Two Babylons, p.11, Rev. A. Hislop, 1916, S.W. Partridge & Co.
[6] The Baltimore Catechism, p.329.
[7] Roman Catholicism, op.cit., p.216.

[8] Sincere Christian, Vol.2, p.68, Dublin, 1783.

[9] The Differences, p.17, booklet compiled by Rev. A. White & Rev. B. Horner, Bible Union of Australia.

[10] The Two Babylons, op.cit., p.10.

[11] Ibid., p.10.

[12] Roman Catholicism, op.cit., p.199.

[13] Shall I Go To Confession?, p.10, (booklet), Rev. W.H. Griffith Thomas, Protestant Truth Society.

[14] Our Priceless Heritage, p.129, H.M. Woods.

[15] I Was A Priest, pp.62-64, L. Vinet, 1949, Protestant Publications.

[16] The Catholic Religion, op.cit., p.136.

[17] The Catholic Encyclopedia, op.cit., p.625.

[18] Our Priceless Heritage, op.cit., p.118.

[19] Notes On The New Testament, p.1387, 1962, Kregel Publications.

[20] A Catholic Catechism For Adults, 1976, Our Sunday Visitor.

[21] Ins and Outs of Romanism, Dr. J. Zacchello, Loizeaux Brothers, New York, 1956.

[22] Shall I Go To Confession?, op.cit., p.9.

[23] I Was A Priest, op.cit., pp.62-67.

[24] Shall I Go To Confession?, op.cit., p.16.

[25] The Priest, The Woman and the Confessional, C. Chiniquy, pp.67,68, The Gospel Witness, Toronto.

[26] The Catholic Bible Has The Answer (booklet), O.J. Smith.

Please Contact:

morenodalbello@yahoo.com.au

Please Visit:

www.godsonlygospel.com

Made in the USA
Monee, IL
08 July 2026

56686376R00024